CREATING VALUE

Your 90 Day Plan
To Right Tracking Your Career

by

Joey D. Havens, CPA,

♦

Dr. Joseph S. Paul

authorHOUSE™

1663 Liberty Drive, Suite 200
Bloomington, Indiana 47403
(800) 839-8640
www.AuthorHouse.com

First published by AuthorHouse 02/18/05

ISBN: 1-4208-1631-4 (sc)

Library of Congress Control Number: 2004099378

Printed in the United States of America
Bloomington, Indiana

This book is printed on acid-free paper.

DEDICATION

To Mom and Dad who not only taught me the importance of strong character and Christian values but lived them everyday. To my wife and partner in life, Cathy, who encouraged me every "page of the way" to complete this book.   -Joey Havens

    With humility and love I dedicate this work to my family, my students, co-workers and clients past and present for all you have taught me through the years; and especially to my Master teachers Aubrey Sanford and Hyler Bracey.   –Joe Paul

ACKNOWLEDGEMENTS

For over 20 years, I have had the honor to work with and be an integral part of a great firm, Horne CPA Group (Horne, LLP). Many of the challenges we faced as we grew the Firm into one of the largest in the Southeast, provided the lessons shared within this book. Thanks to all of the professionals who entrusted their careers to us for advancement, guidance and development. Thanks Roy Ward for your dedicated leadership within the Firm over those years. Our partners are simply the best and none more loyal or dedicated than Greg Anderson who has worked side by side with me for 13 years. Denise McCloud, my administrative assistant, you are simply the best.

Without my co-author Dr. Joe Paul, this book would not have been possible. He has not only made great contributions to this book but has also been a fantastic friend, teacher and confidant. I have learned so much from you. A special thanks to Dr. Hugh Parker and Erin Granberry who not only labored through rough drafts and provided so many great insights and improvements for the book, but also cheered us on to the finish line. Thanks to Shawn McGregor, Shannon Harvey, Julie Tatum and Mandy Thompson who all helped make this book a reality.

The love and support of my family is simply remarkable. My wonderful wife Cathy, Mom & Pop Joe, our children Brandon, Haley, Kelsey, and Rigby, my brother Mike and sister Mitzi, my wonderful in laws James and Happy Cole, and all the rest of the gang. Thanks so much for being there for me and picking me up when I fall. I'm so blessed to have each of you and I love you.

Most of all thanks to God for blessing me so abundantly and providing me with such a rewarding life. God bless you and God bless America!

Joey D. Havens

INTRODUCTION

 Ever think of yourself as running your own personal company?

You really are running your own personal company. This concept is simple but very empowering. Whether you are a new graduate or a professional with twenty-five years of experience, recognizing and understanding this concept can empower you to create tremendous value that will put your professional career on the right track.

This book is designed to assist you in recognizing that you, as a professional, are running your own personal company and that this company's success (your success) will be determined by the amount of time and resources that you invest in yourself. That investment will then grow according to the values you set for your company. The professionals who understand and grasp this concept are empowered to right-track their professional careers from Day One. It is one of the most powerful concepts for you to understand as a professional.

If you will invest a couple of hours in your personal company and learn about the 13 principles of creating value that we have disclosed in this book, you will dramatically increase your effectiveness, your self-confidence, and your satisfaction. And, above all, you will find the right track for your professional career. You will do great things when you take ownership of your company and implement a plan of action that is based upon the 13 principles of creating value.

The wonderful irony is that in today's knowledge and service economy, the more you think of yourself as self-employed and running your own company, the better you serve your employer and your customers. This creates the ultimate Win/Win!

Whatever your chosen profession - attorney, physician, banker, accountant, librarian, architect, engineer, marketing professional - you are working in a fast-paced information age. The value you create in today's market place is based upon your ability to access knowledge, retain knowledge, create new knowledge, and implement that knowledge through teamwork with other professionals.

We are knowledge workers today! As a knowledge worker, you have the ability to increase your value and to create more value as you learn and gain more experience. As a knowledge worker, you have the power to walk away from one enterprise and plug into another enterprise overnight. The flexibility and marketability you have, as a knowledge worker, is unbounded. Technology provides you the ability to remain connected and mobile, as well as to create value from any location in the world, including your own home!

What is the most valuable asset for a company in today's information age? People. That's right, people. Team members will continue to be the most valuable resource for your company. Whether interacting with team members or customers, your people skills, relationship building and networking will ultimately determine the value you create within your company.

Challenging deadlines, demand for specialization, thirst for immediate results, overflow of information, urgent demands, conflicting priorities, changing technologies and complex human interactions all muddy the waters when it comes to mapping out a professional career. Sometimes we get overwhelmed before we even get started. Exhaustion can quickly become the name of the game. You are challenged more today than ever before.

 Creating value principles can assist you in empowering yourself to take control of your career and guide your personal company in the direction and at the speed that best matches your needs and goals. This is what we mean by "right track", a career of empowerment that matches your values and vision for yourself. For some that will be a fast track while others may choose a slower pace. The key is to not wait for things to come to you but recognize what creates value and make it happen in your personal company.

"Even if you're on the right track; you'll get run over if you just sit there."

-Will Rogers

What is Creating Value for a Professional?

How do you create value as a professional? As you hear people talk about results and productivity, what does it mean to you? What is production and how do you define it to set goals for your career?

We have classified creating value (productivity) for a professional into four areas. You do not have to be outstanding in all four areas to have a successful career. You do have to be proficient in all of these areas and outstanding in at least one or two of them.

The most obvious area of creating value is in providing direct customer service. Professionals are best evaluated on their ability to bring solutions and value to the customers they serve. Your time spent on customer projects is a big part of creating value. Some professional firms target this time as the number one factor in compensation and promotions. Customer service includes not only the direct time spent on the account or engagement, but more importantly the results that include information and knowledge to be provided to the customer as a result of those efforts. Good people skills and the ability to work with your team and customer personnel are key to being effective at customer service and ultimately creating value for the customer. Professionals that become outstanding at providing customer service have outstanding careers.

The most overlooked area of creating value is the development of other team members. Although overlooked, this is the greatest challenge professional firms face today! Most professional firms are not putting enough resources into or emphasis on this aspect of their business. But, team development becomes more crucial as you take a leadership role on your team. Leverage is so important to a successful professional firm and that is only obtainable with good people development. One reason this is such a big challenge today, is the ease with which professionals can take their knowledge and move into another organization. Team members want to be trained and challenged as they grow. Aren't you most motivated when you are presented not only with a challenge, but also with the resources to meet that challenge? Accordingly, the most successful leaders in professional firms do an outstanding job of team member development and sharing of knowledge. You cannot lead or grow into a leadership role in a professional services organization unless you can gain the trust and loyalty of your team members. This trust and loyalty starts with your caring about the individual member's success and development. Although the most overlooked aspect of creating value, this is one of the most important where outstanding results bring outstanding rewards.

An important part of team member development is succession planning, or sharing your network and relationships with other team members. Frequently, the concept of succession planning is associated only with the idea of retirement, but succession planning is far more important than that, and should receive considerable attention throughout your career. For example, to provide for people leverage on your customers you need to involve senior, as well as junior team members. Facilitating relationships between the customer and other team members helps cement the overall relationship between the customer and your firm, and fostering these relationships provides the customer with access to solutions when you are unavailable. Having these relationships established is very important as you prepare to move into another area of practice or even retire. If you have not been successful in transferring relationships within your practice, then what long-term value have you created for the firm? This process must start early on as you manage customer relationships and work with other professionals on issues involving these customers. Getting the customer the right solution or creating the right leverage on a project usually involves your ability to use your team as a resource and involve them with the customer. Good succession planning is extremely important as you take leadership roles that may leave you with less time for direct customer work, or as you consider transfers to other cities, or even transfers to other niches within the firm. By starting this process early, you will be creating value for your firm much sooner, and you will be minimizing the risk to both you and the customer if unexpected changes within the firm occur. This planning is what providing long-term value is all about.

Like customer service and team development, marketing is always near the top of the list in any discussion of the important factors professionals should master in order to create value. Rainmakers (team members who regularly bring in new business) are highly valued and sought after by professional service firms. These individuals have developed the expertise, people skills and networks to bring the lifeblood of new business to the organization. A professional service firm must grow to provide opportunities to its team members, and if you can open customer doors for the firm, you will be highly regarded as a professional.

Even if you are not a rainmaker, you need to be good at some aspect of marketing. Since sales are not everyone's cup of tea, you may want to focus on a different type of marketing. The good news is that you can create value in marketing without being a rainmaker. In this sense, one aspect of good marketing starts with providing noteworthy customer service and expanding customer relationships. Some professionals bring significant value to the firm by managing existing relationships and helping expand those relationships to include other services. This kind of marketing is important because most firm growth depends on maintaining and expanding existing relationships, and this expansion is typically most profitable. Another aspect of good marketing that creates value requires you to become the expert with the solutions your client needs. By becoming the recognized expert in an area of your practice (niche), such that your team or customers seek you out for solutions in this area, you bring significant marketing value to the firm. In addition, many times this expertise is a competitive advantage that may influence a new customer to come aboard or an existing customer to remain or request a new service. Taken together, the message is that every professional must recognize that marketing is the lifeblood of a professional firm. Even if you think you may not have the potential to become a rainmaker, there are other ways to market, either by expanding existing customer relationships or developing an identifiable expertise.

The last area of creating value is innovation. As we stated in the introduction, you are working in the information age and change is more rapid than ever before. Therefore, you can create exceptional value for your customers and team members by looking forward and planning, anticipating these changes. What is the next challenge for the customer or your firm? What changes are going to affect the profitability or viability of the customer? What new services are needed to provide the right solutions for customers? Professionals who bring new solutions and create new knowledge for the customers and team members are extremely valuable. Just finding better processes brings value to the team. Firms cannot be successful today by doing what they were doing two years ago or even last week. Professionals that grasp this challenge and become innovative in all processes and services will fast track to success.

In addition to providing the four value areas identified, customer service, team development, marketing and innovation, each professional must also display solid corporate and personal citizenship. Many firms will no longer tolerate a "lone ranger attitude," regardless of the team member's ability to create value in the other four areas. If team members are not good citizens and pleasant to work with, they just do not belong on the team. As the managing partner of large regional accounting firm once stated, "It doesn't make them a bad person, it just makes them not here." Good citizenship will not create significant value, but bad citizenship will certainly reduce any value you have created. Good citizenship requires not only using good people skills, but also performing those administrative functions that are necessary to properly manage the firm. Other aspects of good citizenship include respecting all of your team members and honoring their time as highly as your own; meeting your commitments with team members and being on time and present for team meetings; and presenting a good attitude on a consistent basis. The 13 principles of creating value within this book are a great guide to being a good citizen.

 In short, there are many ways to create value and be productive in your professional career. In all of these areas -- customer service, team member development, marketing, innovation, or good citizenship -- you need to be highly skilled. In addition, your skills need to be outstanding in one or two of these areas. You cannot afford consistently bad, or even average, reviews in any of these value areas and expect to have exceptional long-term success.

Over time, as your professional career grows and your role changes within the firm, you will discover that you need to shift your emphasis on one or two of these value areas to create the most value for you and your team. Plan your development with these key focus areas for creating value and use the creating value principles described herein to help you put an action plan to your professional development.

Each of the following chapters will focus on one of the creating-value principles. Make a note of action steps you can take in the next 90 days to improve upon your strengths within each and every principle. By implementing a 90-day plan that you review and reassess every 90 days, you can and will create phenomenal results with a career that has professional successes as well as personal balance. This discipline and planning will separate the great from the average. Always remember as you apply these principles, to do so within the framework of prioritizing spiritual, personal and professional goals. Balance is critical to your long-term success.

Contents

CHAPTER ONE

CREATING VALUE

COMMITMENT

Your career is a marathon, but the track consists of both flat pavement where you can sprint as well as hills and valleys where you will have to pace yourself. Too many times professionals treat their careers as though they are only a 100-yard dash. To have long-term success in your professional career, you must have commitment. By adopting a mindset of perseverance and endurance, the ups and downs which we all have in our professional careers are much more manageable, helping us to realize that they are only hills and valleys in what is a long race for the finish line. The good news is that we should celebrate those victories and successes along the way, yet we must also exhibit discipline by continuing to invest in and regenerate our company (ourselves) to provide the greatest value to our customers and team. Because commitment requires such effort over the long haul, we find that commitment easier to obtain when we focus on things about which we are passionate.

Passion is so easy to see. The Horne CPA Group hired a young professional several years ago in one its southern Mississippi offices. This young man had been working for the company approximately four to six weeks, when there was a hurricane in the Gulf that caused extensive damage 60 miles inland in Hattiesburg, MS. Electricity was out over most of the town and there were trees down, etc. The shareholder in charge of the office went in about 8:15 that morning to check on the building. Upon arrival he met this young professional, just driving in. He had driven about 30 minutes through the debris to get to the office. A commute that usually takes ten minutes. He was dressed in his best business attire. (We can only assume he had taken a cold shower and shaved in the dark). He was so passionate about his new career that even the hurricane did not slow him down. The team laughed about this together for several years, but always remembered his extraordinarily high level of commitment and passion. Now, it may be unrealistic for us to set this level of commitment as a standard of passion and commitment for our careers, but we can learn from this young accountant that our actions always demonstrate our level of commitment. Good things happen when you are committed and passionate.

It is also our experience that although a successful career requires commitment, discipline and sacrifice, it also requires good balance. Good balance is typically derived from your commitment to a strong set of values, which reflect your personal and spiritual needs. This balance then allows you to weigh family priorities with your professional aspirations.

 Commitment is more a mind set than an action. It is locking in to the lofty goal of creating rare value for those you serve: your customers, your employer and ultimately yourself. It is demonstrated in assuming full responsibility for the results you create. It is marked by a tireless determination and perseverance. Commitment means never giving up and never giving in. Winston Churchill said it best *"Never, never, never give up!"* It is about becoming intentional in learning something from every experience. It is going the extra mile and never being satisfied until the solution is found and value is added. It is not just about trying hard, but rather about creating inspired results. This inner drive separates the "leaders" from the "followers." Commitment is noted by your loyalty to your team, your customers, and your employer while honoring your values.

You must truly believe with all your heart and soul that you can create extraordinary value for those you serve. At our core, most of us truly care about doing good work in the world and being successful in our endeavors. True commitment requires us to uncover this core and dare ourselves everyday to push beyond the comfortable, beyond the ordinary. Fear of failure limits commitment. Approach each day without fear. Ask yourself, "What is the best thing that can happen today if I show uncommon commitment and passion for my work?" You can and will create more value for your company!

COMMITMENT 90-DAY ACTION PLAN

Work through the questions below. Take an honest assessment of your current level of commitment to creating value, and create action steps to move yourself toward 100 percent personal commitment. The time is now!

(a) Rank order the statements below from (1) the statement that best describes you to (6) the statement that least well describes you:

1. I do my part.
2. I am patient in waiting for opportunities to advance my career.
3. I am not ready to move forward professionally.
4. I am preparing for a successful future.
5. The future is now; I am seizing opportunities daily.
6. I can create the professional conditions I need for success.

Your goal is to make statements 4,5 & 6 the ones that best describe you.

If you were to increase your level of personal commitment, what would it look like? What kinds of behaviors would you display? What kinds of actions would you take?

Examples might include:
** I am getting up earlier each morning, energized to make things happen.
** I review my goals each day and prepare a daily action plan.
** As appropriate, I share my level of commitment in speaking with colleagues and clients.
** I ask for help when I need it.
** I openly show my passion for what I do.

In the space below describe three behavioral descriptors that you are committed to living over the next 90 days:

1. _____

2. _____

3. _____

CHAPTER TWO

cREATING VALUE

RISK

Be a risk taker. Professionals who never make mistakes seldom accomplish great things. If you are pushing forward, you are going to make some mistakes. These mistakes are simply an important part of the learning process, and you must create a mindset where making a mistake within your company is OK. The goal is to learn from that mistake and apply that knowledge as you move forward.

Risk taking can be boiled down to two words, "making decisions." Having the confidence to assess the situation, look at the facts and make a decision - that is the task of a true risk taker. Too many professionals fear making a mistake and thus procrastinate when making decisions. Risk takers figure out what needs to be done before being told what to do. They offer solutions for obvious problems to their team and customers rather than excuses or complaints. Good decision makers gather the facts and make decisions in the face of uncertainty. Today's changing environment doesn't allow time for prolonged analysis and lengthy information gathering. Make decisions; it's that simple. You won't stump your toe if you are standing still, but you won't move forward with your career either.

Companies and professionals will not be successful doing the same things they have been doing for the last 20 years. Your job is to challenge the status quo - to always search for a better way. "We've always done it that way" is a sure sign of a company or a professional that is headed for trouble. Being creative with a passion for innovation and a willingness to change are true signs of risk takers who will continue to create value for their company. The reason more professionals are not more creative and innovative is that creativity and innovation take many professionals out of their comfort zones where they may fail. In fact, for you to apply the thirteen principles of creating value, you will have to step out of your comfort zone.

Early in Joey's career, He came up with the idea that they could leverage the tax practice by becoming involved in electronic filing for tax refunds on small individual tax returns. He developed the name "Quick Tax." As it turns out, the venture was too early for the market and his company was not positioned correctly to provide the resources and locations to bring in the necessary volume. In other words, it flopped! To this day, his fellow partners will still bring up "Quick Tax" for some good professional heckling. "Quick Tax" flopped, but it branded Joey as a risk taker, and he learned from his mistake. The company has experienced many successes since then because they encourage innovation and risk taking. There is no doubt that "Quick Tax," although an economic failure, brought about positive results, encouraging Joey to be a risk taker and letting him learn from the experience.

We all like our comfort zone. Here is how Joey relates his experience of expanding your comfort zone. *"Being pushed out of my comfort zone also taught me to stretch professionally. When I stood in front of about 150 seminar participants at my first national presentation on a health care topic, I was a fish out of water! Talk about being out of your comfort zone!!! Each breath was a chore. I'm sure I was a very average speaker, but I survived and learned. I learned a lot more than the participants, and best of all they asked me back the next year. Taking this risk helped launch a great career in health care consulting and continues to open doors even today. Had I never pushed myself out of my comfort zone, these opportunities would have never been available to me."*

You have an opportunity to push yourself in several aspects of your career. You will only grow professionally when you stretch outside your comfort zone whether your fear is public speaking, writing, leading or questioning.

This unwillingness to leave a comfort zone may explain why so many professionals stay on a slower track in their careers. Because they are not comfortable taking risks and investing in and running their own companies, these professionals may find it difficult to excel. Ultimately, you are the decision maker for your company. While risk taking can be daunting, it is riskier not to take any risks. Don't run from risks or mistakes. Don't run from decisions. Assume that responsibility and continue to push yourself to be creative and innovative. Continue to challenge the status quo. Learn from your mistakes. Reward yourself when you have clearly pushed beyond your comfort zone.

We are not suggesting that you can create rare value by throwing all caution to the wind and flailing away trying outrageous things without forethought. Taking risks for the sake of taking risks is not the answer. We are suggesting; however, that you proactively search for opportunities where judiciously stepping out on a limb and doing things differently may produce positive results for your customers or your firm. One well-known definition of insanity is doing the same things over and over and expecting different results. Don't let fear of failure cause you to keep repeating the same actions and prevent you from trying a new approach.

One way to increase your willingness to take risks is to create high-trust relationships with your team and clients. The higher the trust among team members, for example, the more willing the team tends to be to take a shared risk. To foster trusting relationships, share your ideas for innovation openly, and listen carefully as you solicit feedback. Work to develop trust (see Chapter Five) through developing a strong consistency between what you say and what you do. And when you do take a risk that backfires, work doubly hard to clean up the mess and find the right solution. Also remember as you move into more risk taking, the "no surprises" axiom. Folks we work with generally do not like surprises. When trying something new, be forthcoming. Let people know up front what you are doing and why you are doing it.

Start slow. Take those small risks in order to build your way toward bold consistent, decisive risk taking. Instead of just looking at risk/liability (what could happen if this doesn't work), look first to risk/reward (what kind of extraordinary value could be created if this innovation does work). Push yourself to get out of your comfort zone so often, that you are not comfortable staying there! And most importantly, make every risk you take a learning opportunity. Systematically review what worked and what did not work, and apply your learning to the next opportunity. Empower your company to succeed by making decisions.

RISK 90-DAY ACTION PLAN

(a) Respond to these statements to help you discern where you are as a risk taker. Rank order how well each describes you (1- very close; 6-not me at all)

  1. I am most comfortable working in my comfort zone and rarely offer suggestions.
  2. I would rather be an early follower than a leader, learning from others' mistakes.
  3. I have trouble making decisions.
  4. It is exhilarating to try new things.
  5. I pride myself on being an innovator.
  6. I view short-term failures as steps toward finding the best solution.

We want to see you gravitate toward the descriptors in 4, 5, and 6.

(b) Reflect on the past 6 to 12 months in your professional life. Focus on opportunities you had to take a risk that you may have passed on. What stopped you from taking the risk? What outcome resulted? What might have happened if you had tried something new?

(c) Think deeply about the clients and work that are before you over the next 90 days. Where might there be a relatively safe opportunity to take a risk and innovate?

List below at least three specific work-related "risks" you fully intend to take over the next 90 days. Remember a risk can be simply suggesting a solution or decision to a present challenge. Try to be very specific in your description:

Risk #1 _____

Risk #2 _____

Risk #3 _____

CHAPTER THREE

CREATING VALUE

EFFECTIVENESS

Success is all about results, results, results. Efforts are wonderful, but results will create value for you, your company, your employer, your team, and your customers. It is so easy as a professional to be "busy" at work. The problem is that too many professionals are busy with low-priority, low-value activities. A friend of ours says that, "trying is a way of failing noisily." Efforts are noble, but results are what really count in your professional career.

We see many professionals who are efficient. They are organized and in general don't waste much time. Many of these professionals work long hours and still get mediocre results. While being efficient is important, it does not make you effective. It's amazing how truly successful professionals can work fewer hours and generate results that far outdistance those of other very competent professionals who work more hours. What is the difference? Focusing on high value activities and reducing interruptions and distractions. It's not about becoming robotic; you just have to be smart about where you direct your best energy.

Results come from a strong focus and uncommon persistence. As we discussed in the introduction challenging you to implement a 90-day action plan, as you develop the ability to truly focus you will begin to see the results you want. For many professionals, being able to focus begins with good time-management skills. We encourage you to spend the time and resources to purchase and read a time-management book and/or attend a time-management course. Every professional gets 24 hours a day, 1,440 precious minutes, and that never seems to be enough. Time is the great equalizer, but with good time management skills and prioritizing the high value tasks, you can and will turn time into a tool that will help you focus and prioritize appropriately.

 To manage your time is to manage your life. The choices you make about how you spend each moment are critical. Time management is not just about efficiency, but rather effectiveness. Ideally, you should spend 80 to 90 percent of your time on the top 20 percent of your professional priorities. In fact 80% of the value you create for your company will come from the top 20% of your activities. It makes sense to understand what these high value activities are. The idea is not to work harder than the competition, but to work smarter. Effectiveness is about being cognizant of and intentionally focused on your work over the measure of time. Your objective should always be to exceed the expectations of those you serve both in terms of the quality of the service product you provide and the timeliness of its delivery.

Are you playing office or really creating value with your time management? There are many good time-management concepts. We want to share a few with you that have made profound differences in our careers, as well as the careers of many other successful professionals. Creating value for your company takes commitment. It starts with being a good steward of the limited time we all have. Consider some of these concepts to generate extraordinary value for your company and empower yourself to right track your career.

1. Schedule quiet-time for big tasks around high-energy periods. We all have certain times of the day when our energy tends to peak, and we can generate a lot of focus and creativity in these time periods. During these periods of time, external time seems to become irrelevant due to the focus. A great illustration of the power of focus is light. The sun generates thousands of kilowatts of light, which most of us can tolerate easily with some sunscreen. However, if we take a low intensity light source like a laser and focus it on an object we can literally burn a hole through it. Now that is the power of focus. Obtaining focus in your daily routines will bring tremendous value to you. It is the difference in being effective versus efficient.

    This high-energy time is your greatest value-added time. You must recognize it, capture it and utilize it to provide great results and value.

2. Touch paper once. Trash it, execute it, put it in your read file, but do your best to touch paper once.

3. Open e-mails once and above all, do not treat e-mails as urgent. As stated earlier, it is easy as a professional to be busy and many professionals waste two to three hours a day by attending to e-mails and allowing e-mails to interrupt their most creative thought processes. The E-mail alert is one of the biggest time wasters and distractions you can have. Cut it off!!! Use e-mail as a tool and do not allow it to be a constant interruption of your focus.

4. Utilize a "to-do" list every day and prioritize your value added tasks. Remember most of your value and effectiveness comes from the top 20 percent of our activities and tasks. A "to-do" list should be flexible and you may need to re-prioritize several times a day to make sure you stay focused on what is important and not just urgent. Use a method and to-do list that works for you. There is no secret method here besides prioritizing important tasks for better focus. It should be your special system. The ability to prioritize tasks and then focus on results determines the difference in an outstanding career and an average one.

5. When you are groggy or just not having your best day, take a break, go out on a walk, get a snack, do something to regenerate and create a higher level or energy. You will be amazed at your ability to focus better after taking this break.

6. Do the hardest thing first. Sometimes our progress is hampered because we are creating a lot of stress and anxiety over something that we don't want to do or that will be difficult to do. Attack those difficult items first. Joey has a great tip for making phone calls. *"I try to group my calls into specific times each day so I have fewer interruptions. But early in my career, I always made the easy calls first. Many times, I let that difficult phone call stress me or reduce my focus all day because it was there waiting on me, always in the back of my mind. Too frequently, it had a way of worming itself on the next day's to-do list so I had all that misery to look forward to again. Now I make the tough calls first. This builds momentum and my effectiveness has improved dramatically."*

11

7. Review and critique the effectiveness of your workday at its conclusion. Note triumphs and wastes of time. Resolve to attack priorities when you answer the bell the next day. When you have a great day of focus reflect on it. What helped you achieve that high level of performance? We all have bad days. A difference between great results and mediocrity is good management of bad days. Recognize them early on and fight through them. Work on generating some energy and some intervals of focused time. You may need to start with something fun to get the blood flowing. Recognize it and empower yourself to deal with it.

These time management skills will take you a long way toward accomplishing your goals and minimizing or eliminating procrastination. Again, efforts are a important, and you definitely should prepare to expend significant effort, but the bottom line is that the rewards go to the professionals who make a difference and generate outstanding results. That requires focus and persistence.

EFFECTIVENESS 90-DAY ACTION PLAN

Effectiveness is measured in business outcomes. You will know you are effective when you exceed your clients' expectations, when team members request you on the team, when team members seek you out for help, when you are asked by clients for repeat business, when your portfolio of services to those clients grows, when your clients begin to refer others to you, and when you receive faster promotions and larger raises.

(a) In this chapter we talked about the time tested "80/20" rule. The notion is that we would be well served to spend 80 percent of our quality time on the top 20 percent of our business priorities. This rule is tried and true, but it presumes that we have identified our top business priorities.

List below ten primary priorities you see in your work over the next 90 days. Then circle the two most important ones. This represents what you want to spend 80 percent of your highest quality time on! You might follow the same exercise regarding your client list. Who are your top customers? How can you spend more quality time creating value for them?

Top Ten Work Priorities (In Rank Order)

1. _____   6. _____

2. _____   7. _____

3. _____   8. _____

4. _____   9. _____

5. _____   10. _____

What specific strategies can you deploy in the next 90 days to spend more quality time on the top two priorities above:

80/20 Strategy _____

(b) We talked about the value of time management to effectiveness in Chapter Three. What specific time management tools do you intend to use over the next 90 days. Be very specific:

TOOLS:. _____

_____

_____

(c) Our ability to maximize personal effectiveness is sometimes hampered by short-term "urgent" matters of the day. Stephen Covey, in "The 7 Habits of Highly Effective People," described work tasks as those that are urgent and important; tasks that are important but not urgent; tasks that are urgent but not important; and some are neither urgent nor important. One approach is to recognize these tasks and then work on them in priority: urgent and important first; important but not urgent second; urgent but not important third; and not urgent or important last (if at all!).

Thinking of your major tasks over the next 90 days, label them 1-4 based on the above criteria as shown below. Resolve to spend 80 percent of your best time and energy on Cells One and Two.

Cell One - Urgent and Important
Cell Two - Important but not Urgent
Cell Three - Urgent but not Important
Cell Four - Not Urgent or Important

The rare value comes from being able to get more time focused on Cell Two. That is where exceptional value comes from.

List 90 day goals to have make uninterrupted focus time on cell two:

_____

_____

_____

CHAPTER FOUR

CRE**A**TING VALUE

ATTITUDE

Have you noticed how people tend to migrate toward those who consistently have a positive, upbeat attitude? How does your attitude compare? How would customers and other team members describe your attitude on a day-to-day basis?

 Too many professionals fail to realize the effect of their attitude on their family, their team members and their customers. In fact, your attitude can have a dramatic effect, both positive and negative, depending on how you consistently carry yourself and interact with others. Your attitude will ultimately determine your ability to create extraordinary value within your company.

It seems we all know a positive attitude when we encounter one, and negative ones are certainly easy to point out; but at its essence, what is an attitude? Attitude is, at its core, a judgment that others attribute to us based on their interactions with us over time. If you wish to change your attitude, or how others perceive you, focus on changing your interactions, demeanor and the "front door curb appeal" you present through your expressions and body language. Practice smiling. Work overtime at making eye contact with those you encounter. Be a possibility thinker. When approached by others for assistance, try to find a starting place that says, "How can I help this person achieve their goals." Be a "yes until no" person, instead of a "no until yes" person. This may be one of the areas of interpersonal relations where you need to "fake it until you can make it." During those times when you are stressed, distracted or down; try extra hard to present yourself with a smile, listen even more intently with others, and be a bit slow to share your worries and burdens with them.

By displaying a positive, "can do" attitude, you will quickly become a resource for team members, as well as customers. By exuding a combination of self-confidence and passion for what you do, people will quickly become attracted to you. The fastest way to grow a network of team members and customers is with a positive attitude. Another powerful attribute of positive "can do" attitudes is that they are very contagious. It is amazing that when you display a positive "can do" attitude, many of your team members, as well as customers, will adopt that same attitude.

Maintaining that positive attitude is certainly most difficult when plans go wrong or when someone disappoints you. The key here is to keep cool, maintain your temper, and wait until you have become calm before confronting someone who has disappointed you or before reacting to unexpected changes in the plan. While it is easy to let a bad day define your attitude, don't.

We sometimes forget how blessed we are as Joey relates in this personal story. "*I have always prided myself on being positive and upbeat, which is much easier when things are going relatively smoothly. Recently, my Aunt Katie was stricken with cancer and I had the opportunity to visit with her at the hospital. She was reflecting on challenges in her life and specifically her "special needs" son who at the age of 25 has been cared for by her everyday of his life. She related her devastation and anger to me upon first hearing his diagnosis. After this initial shock, she began to realize what a blessing her child was and thanked God everyday for blessing her with this child. Aunt Katie is now using this same positive attitude in her battle with cancer. Given her example, when things go awry, it doesn't take much reflection to get my attitude back on track.*" You probably have a similar personal situation, which upon reflection, helps remind us how blessed we are and helps keep our problems in the proper perspective. These personal reflections can usually help restore some sense of positive attitude to most professional situations.

It is difficult to have a positive attitude without some measure of self-confidence, which by definition allows us to feel good about ourselves. And, while self-confidence is an important part of your attitude, it should be tempered with humility and openness. Focus on being humble in your day-to-day interactions with other team members or customers. It is also important to recognize when we are being stubborn versus having self-confidence in our decisions.

And learn to laugh at yourself. By recognizing our own limitations and being able to laugh at our own mistakes, we invite others to see us as approachable. Several years ago Joey found himself in a very embarrassing situation. *"I was making a presentation in Las Vegas. Immediately prior to the time for my presentation, I had to go to the restroom. Nerves of course!!! The zipper on my pants got stuck, and I could not get my pants zipped. I went into a full panic followed shortly by a slight rage. Realizing I only had three or four minutes before I would be introduced, I had completely lost my positive attitude and self-confidence. I stopped for a moment and reflected on the situation and began to laugh a little at my predicament. As I began to laugh at myself, I relaxed enough to get my pants zipped and arrived in time for my introduction."* Never, ever underplay the importance of laughing at yourself. Successful professionals know how to laugh at themselves.

Would a little laughter help you create more value for your company? Does your attitude create value or destroy value for your company? Based on your management of your attitude, would you pay additional value for your company? A Good attitude will create more value for your company and keep your career on the right track.

ATTITUDE 90-DAY ACTION PLAN

Try to imagine yourself in the shoes of your co-workers, bosses and your clients. Imagine those people interacting with you on a daily basis. How do you think they would describe your attitude? Sullen, gloomy, dismal, laid back, steady, solid, positive, upbeat, energetic, cheerful? Where do you honestly believe you would fall on this continuum as viewed through the eyes of others?

Do you know of any professionals who wake up in the morning, look in the mirror, and resolve to display a poor attitude all day long? Probably not, but it is so easy to get trapped in a situation that we allow to pull us down into the depths of a bad attitude. Sometimes we don't even realize we are there. Maybe you heard about a colleague who received a raise or bonus where you believed you outperformed them. Maybe you were stinging from a comment made by a supervisor, client or team member. Perhaps you feel that your good efforts are going unrecognized. Maybe something at home is distracting you. All of these and many more issues can serve as heavy anchors that pull us down and make us feel stuck in the depths of a gloomy attitude.

(a) The key to unfettering yourself is to, first, recognize the anchor, and, second, do something about it. There are anchors or issues that we can control; there are others that we can influence, and perhaps some that we cannot control or influence but can let go of or come to accept. Go in search of any anchors that are pulling you down from your optimal positive attitude. Identify them here and discern your level of control and influence over them. Develop a 90-day action plan to remove, confront, influence or release the anchor. Commit your plan to writing and take action.

Action Plan:

Anchor: control-influence-accept-release

1. _____

2. _____

3. _____

(b) Remember that "attitude" is really a perception and judgment that other people hang around your neck based on their evaluation of your behaviors. In the case of attitude, their perception is your reality. You do, however, control your behaviors. Focus on the behavioral areas below and if you feel you need work on them, create a 90-day action plan to do so, starting today!

Smiling vs. Frowning
Positive eye contact vs. Looking Away or Distracted
Energetic vs. Lethargic
Proactive vs. Reactive
Negative vs. positive conversation
Accepting of Uncontrollable Things vs. Sulking
Celebrating vs. Complacency
Laughing vs. Withdrawn

CHAPTER FIVE

CREА**T**ING VALUE

TRUST

We all know how important trust is to any relationship. Managing professional relationships is key in creating value. Few will be the times you can create extraordinary value alone. You are dependent upon significant others to create special results. Making things happen with and through your relationships with other people, whether they are clients, colleagues, subordinates or superiors, is critical to growing your personal company. Dynamic interpersonal skills and trust are crucial. But, the trust of others must be earned; it is typically not given freely. Becoming trustworthy through the quality and integrity of your interactions with others will allow you to create a "low risk" environment, where people are unafraid to suggest or try new ways of doing things. Out of this high trust/low risk environment come great solutions and innovation. Without high levels of trust from those with whom you work, you cannot create extraordinary value as a team member or leader. With high levels of trust you can become a true leader, bringing about higher levels of performance, satisfaction, and success.

In simple terms, we build trust by doing what we say we will. That's it, do what you say you will do. If you promise a customer or team member that something will be done on a certain date at a certain time, then make whatever sacrifices necessary to meet that commitment. One issue that adversely affects trust between parties is reliance on fuzzy agreements. What is a fuzzy agreement? A fuzzy agreement is one in which the two parties to the agreement have a different understanding of the commitment being made. For example, let's assume you had a supervisor or team members ask you to complete a project for them to deliver to the customer next week, which you committed to. Let's also assume this team member did not communicate to you that their meeting was on Wednesday. Since you were scheduled through Wednesday, you plan on completing the project on Thursday. On Wednesday next week, you will find a team member or supervisor who is going to be very disappointed; and yet, that breakdown in communication and subsequently trust was a result of both parties not understanding what the other had committed to. That is a fuzzy agreement. Fuzzy agreements destroy trust. Make your agreements clear, concise and time bound.

Many professionals struggle with their ability to meet their commitments. This struggle often results from a tendency to over-promise, a failure to balance, or a failure to prioritize before making commitments. This struggle becomes even more important when professionals try to balance their personal and professional commitments. One way to keep from over-committing is to learn to say "no" to some of the many requests made of us. It is natural for us to struggle with saying no to someone, particularly someone in a position of authority. There are, however, tremendous demands made on our time and lives, and without learning the skill of saying "no", you will be over-committed, perhaps making yourself miserable and stressed. Sometimes you simply have to say NO.

Another aspect of building trust is to present yourself as being open to challenge and criticism from other professionals. Joey experienced this in his personal development. *"This has always been a struggle for me personally. Too many times in my interactions with team members and customers, I did not appear open enough for them to feel comfortable expressing their true feelings and desires. I had to work on being more open and being a better listener. Feedback is the breakfast of champions."*

So trust comes not only from doing what we say, but also by conveying that we are receptive to other people's feedback, perceptions, needs, and opinions. In developing your spirit of openness, make a conscious effort to practice, especially with team members where you may feel that you don't have as high a trust level as you need. By making yourself vulnerable, you are actually empowering yourself to have more positive impact in the future.

Another great way to build trust with your team members is to share your knowledge and experiences. Early in Joey's career, he was faced with a difficult challenge with a team member who did not trust him. *" Despite all of my efforts to open up and seek input, I could not get this team member to open up and trust me. It was not until I began to share knowledge with him and provide him with all of my resources that he began to respond. This teaching and sharing combined with honoring my commitments to the team won him over. He now leads several team members with very little assistance from me."* For a professional this can be the greatest satisfaction of all, helping others achieve phenomenal results and succeed at creating value. Nothing builds trust faster than helping others. So, be prepared to advise and encourage others as they take risks, suggest new solutions, or challenge the status quo.

One of the greatest destroyers of trust, regardless of how hard you have worked on building that trust, is the failure to respect or honor the confidentiality of others. As you progress, your network grows and your interactions grow. As you report to other professionals and other professionals report to you, you cannot over-stress the importance of confidentiality. In your mentoring relationships, confidentiality is absolutely vital if you expect your mentees to respect you and you want to create an environment through which you can help them succeed. You must respect all of these relationships with a high degree of confidentiality. Keep negative comments about others to yourself. Convert them to constructive feedback at the proper time directly to the individual. Always be open, honest and direct in your evaluations of others.

Realize as you move forward with your 90-day plan, that trust is something that builds over time. Every time you do what you say, you add a stick of credibility to the basket of trust and when you don't do what you say that you spill several sticks from the basket. Building trust takes time. It requires commitment, as we discussed in Chapter One, to stay the course, to realize you are in a marathon, not a 100-yard dash. And that if you are consistent with your commitments, if you don't over promise, you can begin to build trust from Day One. High trust with team members and customers will create more value and empower you to do great things.

<u>TRUST 90-DAY ACTION PLAN</u>

Dynamic leadership is needed to create true value for others. The art of getting things done with and through other people is critical to right tracking and growing your personal company. At its essence, leadership is about influence, and our ability to influence others is dependent upon gaining their trust. As we have stated, trust is earned over time through openness, appropriate self-disclosure, and most importantly by doing what you say you will do with great consistency. Being consistent in keeping your commitments creates credibility, respect and ultimately high trust.

(a) Reflect on the past several months. Are there occasions when you have made commitments to or agreements with others in your work world, that, though well intentioned, you were not able to keep? What effect might this have on your credibility and trustworthiness?

We challenge you to set 90-day goals to increase your consistency in the areas listed below:

1. Making only those commitments and agreements I fully intend to keep.
    Your 90-day goal: _____

2. Learning to consistently, directly and compassionately say "no" when this is the appropriate answer to requests of my time and talents.
    Your 90-day goal: _____

3. Making my agreements and commitments crystal clear and time bound as opposed to "fuzzy" and ambiguous.
    Your 90-day goal:_____

4. Opening myself up to the ideas and feedback of others.
    My 90-day goal: _____

5. Opening up to others, by appropriately disclosing to others more about who I am, what my goals, hopes and dreams are; what I am good at; where I am trying to improve....
    My 90-day goal: _____

CHAPTER SIX

CREATING VALUE

INTEGRITY

Most of us spend years learning to do things right. Often we think too little about learning to do the right thing. But our devotion to doing the right thing, or our integrity, defines us. Accordingly, there can be no compromise for your integrity. If you or your company loses integrity, you will be a loser. And with respect to integrity, it is a given that actions speak louder than words. We can talk a good game about integrity and about doing what is right, but ultimately people will evaluate our integrity based solely on our actions. What you do speaks volumes about who you are and what you believe in. Maintaining your integrity must be your top priority. Again, there is no room for compromise in doing what is right. Another way of stating this is that we all need to do a "gut check" to make sure we are making the right decision sometimes.

Many young professionals, as well as older professionals, do not realize the amount of courage it takes to do what is right. We've seen the disasters in the business world from WorldCom, Enron, Health South, and many others, where leaders, professionals who had the trust of many individuals, did not have the courage to do the right thing. And without a corresponding dose of courage, our integrity can be easily lost.

Integrity affects us in all areas of our life, personally, spiritually and professionally. Our integrity depends on the small things, as well as the big things. Sometimes it is the small actions that don't seem important that can start us in the wrong direction or affect someone's perception of our integrity and character. Whether its skimming your employer on time, giving less than your best efforts, inflating a reimbursable expense or cheating at a golf game, all these activities put your character in jeopardy and can lead to bigger compromises. And, the small gains

25

we achieve are not worth the losses in character that we incur. There is an old saying that there is no such thing as a white lie....A lie is a lie!

While we were writing this book, Joey's firm suffered the tragic loss of one of it's partners, Jobie Melton. Jobie served as Director of Assurance Services and as a board member. The outpouring of support from the community to his family was phenomenal. Over and over we heard about the integrity and honesty of Jobie in his spiritual, personal and professional relationships. Jobie exhibited the highest integrity in all that he did, which defined his extremely successful career. He made everyone around him a better professional and person. Jobie's eulogy was everything he could have wanted it to be, because he directed his life that way.

You are presently writing your own obituary. You have the opportunity to influence the writing of that obituary now and hopefully in the years to come. Think about what you want to stand for and what you want to be remembered for. Make sure you are headed in that direction. Be true to yourself and those around you.

Perhaps the most typical issue of integrity professionals face occurs when customers' expectations conflict with what we know is the right thing to do. In resolving these issues, try first to give the customer the benefit of the doubt even when you feel that they may be taking advantage of you or taking an unfair position. But, this doesn't mean you should sacrifice your integrity for the client. When you find yourself in this situation, red flags and alarms should be going off in your head. This type of pressure has ruined the career of many professionals as they gave into the customer pressure. No customer is worth your integrity.

Nor should you feel obliged to work for just any customer who seeks your services. Before associating yourself with a customer, you need to make a gut check on their integrity. By working with them, you will be associated with their reputation. What is their reputation in the community and their industry? How do they treat their people and their customers? Better yet, how do they treat you and your team members? If you are not in position to make this decision with your employer, you still have a responsibility to give your employer honest feedback on how you feel about the customer and their integrity.

It can be very tempting to compromise our integrity when we have made a mistake or error and we try to cover it up with a half truth or outright lie. Our human nature is to avoid, procrastinate or to even tell the "white lie" to cover up a mistake. Two of the great wastes of our time and energy can be found in the actions of blaming and justifying. Enormous energy and time go into to explaining why the desired result was not reached, or justifying why we fell short of the mark. Imagine the possibilities if you used that time to continue to seek a creative solution to the challenge before you. Even the cover up of small mistakes will dramatically affect your integrity and your ability to build trust and to lead a team of fellow professionals.

Regardless of the situation, always ask yourself "What is the right thing to do?" The earlier you do this in your career, the easier it is to have the courage to do what is right. Perform regular "gut checks" and do the right thing, you will be empowered to do great things.

INTEGRITY 90-DAY ACTION PLAN

Integrity is about unfailing honesty, and about developing and fine-tuning an internal compass that guides you in tough situations. Integrity can be cultivated through the process of identifying your own personal core business and personal values. Our values can be defined as beliefs that are actually acted upon. In this regard, two markers of our internal values are how we spend our time and how we spend our money. You will know the difference between a belief and a value when you find yourself fighting for it. Core values are those issues where you draw the line in the sand and stand strong. In this regard, it is better to have just a few really heartfelt values that you can truly live by, than to have a laundry list of beliefs you cannot live up to.

(a) Reflect on the past year and think of instances when you had the courage to do the right thing under tough circumstances. How did this make you feel and what was the outcome?

_____

(b) Think of instances over the past year where your integrity could have been or was compromised by your actions. How did you feel and what was the outcome?

_____

(c) How can you better prepare yourself to deal with these instances in the future?

_____

(d) Create a list of your core business and interpersonal (how you treat others) values. Remember a value is a belief you will act upon in every circumstance.

_____

Core Values:

1. _____

2. _____

3. _____

4. _____

5. _____

(e) Place your list of core values in a place where you will look at it every day. Keep a journal over the next 90 days of all instances where you acted upon these values.

(f) Take the time to list some things you want to be remembered for in your career and personal life. Use this exercise to reflect on how you are prioritizing things in your life. How will your obituary read?

CHAPTER SEVEN

CREATING VALUE

NICHE

Professionals who build a niche (expertise) ultimately create more value. Customers and employers will pay more value for real expertise. Team members will perceive higher value with expertise. And, in today's marketplace, a niche makes sense for you cannot be all things to all people. In the information age, general information is accessible by everyone and the competition is fiercer than ever. Historically, professionals whether in law, accounting, engineering, banking, whatever the service area, were successful by serving a very wide range of customers with a general array of knowledge. Today that is a recipe for failure or at least mediocrity.

Regardless of your profession, your service area or the industry in which you work, you cannot be all things to all people. Certainly being knowledgeable in many different areas has value, but your goal is to also become the "go to" person in some niche area. All service areas, all industries and all professions offer opportunities to develop a niche. In a law firm, you might develop a niche in a certain aspect of labor law. You might develop a niche of being a great litigator on health care cases. You might develop a niche of being a great researcher. In accounting, although you may be a CPA with a tax emphasis, there is opportunity to develop a niche in a specific aspect of taxation or even taxation within a certain industry such as health care or construction. Begin now to evaluate your areas of interest that would provide opportunities for you to create exceptional value for your customers, employer and your company (self).

 If you read as little as 15 minutes a day, you can be an expert on a subject in three years. It sounds easy, but if it were easy, most professionals would be fast tracking with areas of expertise. It takes focus. It takes discipline. It takes a plan of action. It also takes lots of passion. This devotion of time, energy and resources is why you need to find an area that interests you. Where is your passion? What do you like learning? What areas are fun for you?

You cannot start this process too soon or too late. Again, with a very disciplined program of an hour a day, you can build an expertise in as short as a year to eighteen months. You can become the "go to" person for your team and for your customers. One of the ways your company can continue to create value will be by developing a niche.

As you work on your 90-day plan, stop and reflect on the areas where you find that you are most passionate. Talk to your customers, talk to your team members and identify areas of opportunity for expertise. Look at other professionals in your company or with whom you network and see where they are successful, in what niche areas are they expanding. The most successful professionals typically have a niche they have developed.

Joey was fortunate early in his career to decide to move into a niche area. *"For me that passion and niche was Physician Services and/or the healthcare industry. It quickly became evident that the areas for specialization within this niche were numerous. Therefore, I had to focus on one area of operations. Once I mastered that area, I attacked a second area of operations. That expertise provided me with opportunities to create exceptional value and fast track my career."*

Once you start a niche area, it becomes very difficult to maintain that focus, especially if you have an established professional career with a number of existing customers. Joey also faced with a similar challenge. *"I had worked in tax and audit across several industries including municipalities and governmental auditing. I had built up a number of relationships. As I developed my niche and increased my expertise, my focus was targeted more on those new customers. It became more and more difficult to serve my existing customers. At times, fellow professionals questioned my plan of action. They wondered if I was missing some opportunities by being so focused. However, my goals required that I stay focused on the path that I had chosen. I took that risk. I began to introduce other team members into these existing relationships and migrated my general customer base to other team members. In addition, I quickly trained our customers to call my team members who had additional expertise to meet their needs. This increased our value to the customers and increased my value to our firm. While increasing our firm's value to the client, I became more focused on physician services. Better solutions for our customers led to greater value, longer relationships and higher trust."*

Be the champion in an area. Sometimes you will have to let an opportunity go so that you can be prepared for a bigger opportunity. The days of being everything to everybody have come and gone. Customers and team members are very informed with knowledge readily available in many forms. You need to be the best in at least one area.

FINDING YOUR NICHE 90-DAY ACTION PLAN

Developing a special niche of unique expertise is critical to right tracking your career and creating value. No matter how competent you become in displaying the other principles, cutting edge competence will always be a common denominator to your success. With the explosion of knowledge in today's business environment, you will be hard pressed to be all things to all people. Generalists are giving way to specialists in all areas of the service arena.

(a) What niche areas within your profession have strong upside potential in the short and long term future? Talk to customers and team members about various opportunities for additional expertise. Take notes.

(b) Among those areas, where does your passion rest? Or, in which areas can you envision developing an abiding passion to learn and serve?

(c) Decide now to develop a niche. When that decision is made it is time to get busy. My niche will be_____.

(d) Develop a current reading list of journals, periodicals, and specified length of time each day. Search for seminars, training sessions, teachers and mentors for your learning.

CHAPTER EIGHT

CREATIN**G** VALUE

GROWING

Never ever stop learning and growing. In today's information age, your current skill set diminishes substantially in three years. Information and technology are moving so quickly today, that as a professional you will not maintain your value in the marketplace unless you become a continuous learner. In the past, you could count on your skill set as you gained additional experience to help you provide value for ten or fifteen years. That is not true in today's professional marketplace. The prize goes to those who grow and learn. If you wait until you have experience in an area, you may never become an expert in that field. Opportunities come quicker to those who demonstrate knowledge. Why not empower yourself on your own timetable rather than waiting to see what "might" happen.

 Develop a passion for learning. The star performers develop a discipline for reading. Read, read and then read some more. Remember, by reading 15 minutes a day, you can become an expert on a subject in three years. View continuing education programs not merely as means of keeping your necessary credentials but as an opportunity to expand the value of your personal company. As you mature in your profession, you will have a stronger desire, urgency, even a hunger to develop more knowledge through learning. Staying smart is one of your greatest challenges today!

One of the best ways to meet this challenge is to teach. That's right, to teach others. Taking the opportunities to share within your team or lead a group discussion on a specific topic or engagement will provide you with more knowledge. This teaching can begin in your comfort zone on areas with which you are familiar and with team members. For some, the right track will be only internal sharing and teaching. One on one instruction is very important. Others will find the desire to teach outside of their company to peers and customers. Regardless of the teaching level to which you progress, the sooner you begin to share your knowledge, the quicker you will grow as a professional. Value comes from not only growing yourself but also your customers and team members.

Teaching played a vital role in Joey's personal career and development. *"Having been fortunate to teach at numerous conferences across the country, I quickly learned that my knowledge grew tremendously from these experiences. As a result of teaching and sharing, I learned more than participants. Some of the best experiences for me have always been sharing with my team members. Seeing my team members learn and grow brings a true sense of accomplishment and professional satisfaction."*

Teaching challenges you to grow in two ways: 1) Teaching presents the challenge of knowing that people are looking to you to bring new knowledge and new information to them. 2) The participants bring knowledge and experiences that you may have never discovered on your own. To grow, look proactively for opportunities to teach and share your knowledge with others. It is our experience and belief that this investment returns to you ten fold. With a passion for learning and a willingness to share that knowledge, you can achieve a high satisfaction level and create value as a result of your efforts.

The "light" seems to come on sooner for different people at different times in their careers. Empower yourself with this principle of Growing and turn your "light" on sooner and begin to grow quickly as a professional.

You may find yourself grappling with some common stumbling blocks to growth. Many professionals lose the battle to these stumbling blocks early on and find themselves behind in their career track. By knowing and recognizing these tendencies, you can avoid many of these stumbling blocks. One tendency is to assume that you are the exception to these thirteen principles outlined in this book, rationalizing that the need to grow or the need to read doesn't apply to you. In other words, "I'm different; I'm the exception. I'm smarter than everyone else." No one is an exception. Don't let your self confidence get in the way of true progress. Another stumbling block arises when we impose premature expectations that the information will be of little value or that again it doesn't apply to me. Once you are in this mindset, it is difficult to learn. Another dangerous assumption can be, "I already know all of this, or there is nothing new here."

 One of the scariest stumbling blocks to growth that we have encountered deals with the expectation of entitlement. Too many young professionals start their careers with an attitude that they are entitled to a certain title and career track regardless of their performance. Don't I deserve this? The only real concern exhibited is focused on the next raise or promotion with no consideration of overall performance. These expectations are not realistic in the real business world. You can't wait for your career to come to you. Although any good employer is going to invest in training for you, the primary responsibility for your growth lies with you.

Another stumbling block deals with disliking a team member, leader or presenter. You do not have to like someone to learn from them. We have become an "entertainment" culture today that encourages short attention spans. If we are not "wowed" by the style of a presenter or the content of a written piece within the first few minutes, we tune it out, or turn it off. Recognize when you may be tuning out too quickly and make sure you're doing so for the right reasons, for even a boring presenter may have something to teach you. Try to capitalize on all of your learning opportunities.

Do you ever get overwhelmed or just plain exhausted by the need to learn and manage information? Why do I have to continue to learn? I got my education already. This feeling of being overwhelmed tends to be most noticeable when we get our lives out of balance and do a poor job with our time management. Sometimes you need to take a break and do something just for you. Spoil yourself and renew your energy. In fact this should be part of planning a "right track" for your career. Always balance hard work with lots of hard play and celebrations for goals reached.

The bottom line is that to grow, you must continue to learn. Success follows those who develop that desire to learn and prioritize a commitment to reading.

As you work on your 90-day game plan, explore areas where you have an interest, something about which you could become passionate.

Start reading and researching in your areas of interest. Begin to look for opportunities to use this knowledge or share it with team members. With a small amount of effort you can begin to right track sooner than you might expect. Self-growth will empower you. Goals and timelines that seemed unobtainable will quickly be within your reach.

By making a commitment to yourself, you can take the first step towards professional growth. Why wait until others catch on before you? Seek knowledge and the many opportunities it can afford you. Read a little everyday! Grow and create value with extraordinary results.

GROWING 90-DAY ACTION PLAN

At the conclusion of Chapter Seven, we encouraged you to identify a specialty niche and get busy developing an education plan to become an expert. The "growing" principle gives you the challenge of expanding the Chapter Seven "niche" plan into a more comprehensive personal and professional development plan.

Experience tells us that those who are intentional and relentless in their own continuing education and professional development find the richest success in creating value. You need a comprehensive plan, and a proactive approach to growing the knowledge capacity of your personal company.

In addition to your niche, what areas do you want to grow in? Communications skills? Active listening? Public speaking? Industry knowledge?

(a) Identify below, two or three areas in addition to your niche that you would like to grow your knowledge and skills. These should be areas that you need to reach goals, and areas that you can get excited about.

Areas for growth:

1. _____

2. _____

3. _____

(b) Develop a 90-day "get started" plan for each of the above. Identify resources, readings, experts and seminars or workshops that might help you. Commit to a written plan to utilize these resources over the next 90 days.

Growth plans:_____

(c) The notion that the more you teach others, the more you learn and grow is a powerful one. What opportunities are out there for you to do some teaching? Maybe a brown bag gathering of your colleagues to share knowledge on a new process; a State or Regional conference; a client educational session???

Work hard to identify and create at least one teaching opportunity for yourself over the next 90 days.

Teaching Opportunity:

What _____

When _____

Where _____

Who _____

CHAPTER NINE

CREATING VALUE

VISION

What is a professional career without vision and goals? The answer is about half as successful as one that utilizes a strong vision with stretch goals. It does make a difference. Alice asks the Cheshire cat while wandering lost through Wonderland, "Which way shall I go?" The wise cat replies, "That depends upon where you want to get to." Alice ponders and responds, "I don't quite know where I want to get to." The cat then observes, "Then it does not matter which way you go." Steven Covey calls it "beginning with the end in mind." The Bible says, "Without vision the people shall perish." In this marathon mentality we want to see you develop, you must know where the finish line is. You must see where you want to go and develop an unquenchable desire to get there. Visioning is risky. You may not get where you plan. We challenge you take the risk of envisioning a desired future for your personal company and being about the business of living that vision each and every day. Many professionals spend great time and energy looking for the magic elixir called motivation. Motivation comes from creating a vision so mighty and purposeful that a healthy tension is created within you to work smart and hard every day to reach your destination.

Your vision for your personal company comes to life by setting very specific and challenging goals. Combine this goal setting with action plans and commitments to move you toward the achievement of your vision. This vision with prioritized action plans help to guide your daily choices in terms of how you spend your resources and time. Think of the vision as the fuel that drives the engine. Are you running on empty? Where do you want to be in three, five and ten years? What will your day be like, what will your company look like, how big will your company be, what kind of value will you be creating, what kind of work will you be doing? Creating value begins with a vision.

 In visioning and goal setting, sometimes less is more. It is easy to set too many goals, thus depriving yourself of the energy from being focused. Set a vision that is compelling and real to you. It should be visionary in that you can actually picture it in your mind. Build goals that are clear and measurable. Focus on a few prioritized goals. This exercise will propel you onto the right track for your career. This exercise is very empowering for a professional.

Goals should be created to stretch you and help you out of your comfort zone. Far better to set a lofty goal and fall just short of it than to create an easily reachable one that does not add true value to your endeavors.

We shared with you earlier the sense of achievement and professional satisfaction that comes from helping others get their career on the right track, find success, and/or expand their knowledge. Include goals or plans to help others succeed along the way. Creating value means helping others be successful also.

Only you can hold yourself accountable for meeting your goals. Only you can set the benchmark high enough that you stretch yourself. Stretching yourself will result in creating more value. Chinese Mao Tse Tung may have said it best concerning vision, *"We think too small, like the frog at the bottom of the well. He thinks the sky is only as big as the top of the well. If he surfaced, he would have an entirely different view."* Don't let your vision of your professional career be narrowed by the walls of the well or constraints placed on your professional career. Always climb to the top of the well and look at the full sky. Set your vision and goals based on a full sky.

VISION 90-DAY ACTION PLAN

The immediate work you do on the visioning principle may be the most important of all. It is most difficult to create a desired future without clearly and boldly envisioning it and coming to truly believe you can achieve it. Argue for your limitations and they become your limitations. Expanding your vision of what is possible is a powerful motivator. Knowing where you are going can and will assist you in your daily direction and decision-making.

(a) The time is now for you to create a personal vision statement that is so bold as to be almost embarrassing. The best vision statements describe a future desired reality in the present tense, as though you are already there. Instead of saying, "I aspire to be a nationally recognized expert in the field of nano-widgets. I will be respected within my profession and community and known for creating exceptional value for those I serve," state these bold notions for the future as though you are already there. "I *am* a nationally recognized expert in nano-widgets. I *enjoy* respect within my profession and community. I *create* consistent exceptional value for those I serve. I am a powerful teacher and mentor. My greatest strength is helping others find success along the way." Whatever your vision, make it a mighty one that will stretch you and fulfill you. Your personal vision statement should include what business you are in, what your niche is, what you are really good at, how you treat others, as well the kinds of outcomes you create. Take time now to write your personal vision statement. Remember to write it in the present tense. It should be brief (no more than three or four sentences) and powerful.

Personal Vision Statement_____

(b) Goals, strategies, tactics and ultimately action bring your vision to life. Without a plan to reach it, your vision is merely a wish, a prayer, a dream. The best goals are stated in behavioral terms and include outcomes that are observable and measurable. Goals should be important to you (motivating), specific, measurable or observable, and time bound.

Take time now to develop some specific starter goals to move you toward your vision. Make sure each passes the test of being specific, measurable, observable and time bound.

Major Goals:

1. _____

2. _____

3. _____

4. _____

5. _____

CHAPTER TEN

CREATING vALUE

ACCOUNTABILITY

Please delete from your professional vocabulary the following four words, "I did my part."

As a professional, you cannot just do your part. You have the opportunity to lead, and you can choose to be 100 percent responsible for the results you create. A professional who takes complete responsibility is personally accountable for the outcome of a communication, a project, a meeting or exceeding a customer's expectations. Complete accountability means accepting full responsibility without laying blame or justifying.

When events do not go as expected, many professionals begin trying to justify the unexpected results. For example, some might attempt to justify a poor quarterly result by stating, "We were not profitable last quarter because the economy was in a down turn." While this justification may be factual, when added to the result that you were not profitable, the justification does not change the outcome. A better idea is to develop a mindset that says, "How can we innovate and create a profit in a slow economy?" This mindset recognizes the constraints placed on it by the circumstances, but adjusts for those constraints rather than using them to justify poor performance. Just on the other side of blame and justification, creative solutions and innovations are waiting to be harvested. It's easy in our professional lives to blame some outside event, some other team member, or the lack of cooperation from the customer for an unsuccessful project, a missed deadline, or a miscommunication. True professionals, however, are accountable for the outcome, regardless of the events beyond their control. With true accountability, you take ownership of the process.

 Is taking ownership and being accountable more difficult in your first, second, or third year as a professional? Absolutely, but it is in those years that your actions send a message to your team members that, "Hey, this is someone special. This is someone who gets it. This is someone who has a 'can do' attitude and is personally accountable for everything they touch." When you exhibit personal accountability without blaming others for failures, you will quickly be in demand from team members as well as customers. People are attracted to professionals who take responsibility, make things happen and are accountable for the outcomes.

One of the toughest times to be personally accountable is when we have made a mistake that leads to an unfavorable outcome. It is human nature in this situation to begin finger pointing and justifying, trying to avoid accountability. Instead, be courageous and own up to your mistakes; view the entire process as a way to improve and avoid similar mistakes in the future. By demonstrating your willingness to be held accountable, you can inspire others to work towards better solutions.

Under the principle of Growth in Chapter Eight, we inquire as to who is responsible for our personal development and growth. This is an area where you must not rely on others but assume 100 percent responsibility and take charge of your own development. Don't wait in the back of the bus; get in the driver's seat when it comes to your development as a professional.

In summary, 100 percent accountability is a state of mind in which you do everything within your power to meet expectations. Even when presented with complicating circumstances outside of your control, you continue to lead the search for solutions and follow up with all affected parties to ensure the best possible outcome for everyone. Assuming responsibility and accountability can be a transforming principle for your professional and personal life. While it takes great discipline and creativity, this is a very empowering principle.

ACCOUNTABILITY 90-DAY ACTION PLAN

Assuming 100 percent accountability challenges us to hang in there and be resilient. Accountability means moving away from making excuses and moving toward finding solutions.

As you develop your 90-day plan on the accountability principle, reflect on instances where had you been more accountable for the process there might have been a better outcome. Before setting your accountability plan, answer these questions:

How would you describe the culture and environment where you work relative to blaming and justifying? Is there a lot of it?

How would you assess yourself in terms of the amount of energy and time you exert in blaming or justifying (or making excuses)?

Identify two or three areas that you want to become completely accountability for over the next 90 days. These may be particular projects, work items, clients, etc. By committing you are pledging not to blame or justify, nor just do your part, but rather to assume 100 percent responsibility for creating the outcome you want.

One hundred percent Accountability Pledge List:

1. _____

2. _____

3. _____

Remember never use the phrase "I did my part." If you do catch yourself using this type of logic, do an immediate personal assessment to see why you have chosen to not assume 100 percent responsibility in this situation. What can be learned?

CHAPTER ELEVEN

CREATING VALUE

LISTENING

Listening may well be the most important and the most difficult interpersonal skill you can develop. While most of us understand that communication is a two way street, we focus most of our energy on getting our message across, and far too little energy on understanding the messages being sent to us. Our innate ability to focus on the messages we are sending explains why communication itself is not one of the thirteen principles in creating value. Most of us do a great job of telling everybody our perspective. What we do not do so well is to understand our team member's or customer's perspectives. Listening well is a hard skill to acquire, making it one of the principles of creating value.

Listening was one of Joey's greatest stumbling blocks. *"My greatest weakness as a new professional and new leader within our firm dealt with my inability to effectively listen in order to really understand. I found myself always wanting to form my responses before others had completely expressed their views. On my early performance evaluations, the feedback on "ability to listen to others" was always one of my lowest scores. I took this evaluation to heart and realized listening was a skill I had to develop. With training and hard work, I've improved my ability to listen and thus effectively communicate. Anyone who is willing to work can become a good listener."*

Listening is an active process. It may sound passive, but listening requires more energy and focus than any other part of communication. Like the laser, a low intensity light source that becomes more powerful even than the sun itself when focused, listening becomes a very powerful tool when you actively attend to what is being communicated and focus purposefully on that communication.

You have probably heard of the concept of or experienced listening checks. Maybe, you've even thought someone was a little crazy when they repeated to you what you had just told them. These listening checks, which involve stating back what you think you have just heard, can be great learning exercises and self checks on your listening skills. Just practicing listening checks can be a very useful and important part of the process of training yourself to actively listen. Now, be careful about repeating everything that is said, as some of your associates might begin to look at you a little funny. But paraphrasing what you think you have heard actually sends others a very strong message that you value their thoughts and care about their perspective.

Professionals that are effective listeners have a better understanding of a customer's expectations, and thus they are more successful at meeting those expectations. The easiest place to become lax with our listening is with our team members with whom we interact everyday. Because of this daily interaction, it is often too easy to take these communications or individuals for granted. View each team member as an individual person with unique needs and goals. Focus your internal laser on listening during these interactions. By consistently being a good listener with your team members, you will gain the respect it takes to create value for your company.

 Keep in mind that if listening were easy, everybody would be a good listener. It takes hard work and a strong desire to become a good listener. While we are all tempted by a strong desire to express our own viewpoint, if you want others to buy-in to your position or solution, you must demonstrate that you have heard and understood their views. Understanding the views of others is impossible without effective listening. If you are going to be a leader in your team and with your customers, you must develop a burning desire to be an effective listener with a compelling passion for understanding.

Remembering that we all want to be heard and understood is key to focusing on others. You have to see beyond yourself in order to truly give others the attention they want and need. Steven Covey and others have promoted the notion introduced centuries ago by St. Francis, of "seeking first to understand, then to be understood." What better place, what more important place than the knowledge service environment to seek first to truly understand the perspectives of your customers, colleagues, subordinates and bosses? Don't worry; they will be the first to notice your efforts in this area. Effective listening is key to being on the right track.

LISTENING 90-DAY ACTION PLAN

Listening is, in our opinion, the paramount interpersonal skill. Remember that all of us have a fundamental need and desire to be heard and understood. And nothing earns our respect and trust more readily than the feeling we experience when we have truly been heard and understood. Though communication is a part of most every college curriculum and corporate training program, these programs tend to focus on speaking and presenting. We receive far too little training in the skill of active listening. Active listening helps us discern not only the content of messages but also the affect or emotion within them. At a deep level most of us understand the importance of listening well. Given all of this, why is it so difficult?

(a) Identify your personal barriers to effective listening. For each barrier you list, develop a strategy for overcoming it.

> **Example:** Barrier – "I am too busy thinking about my response to listen well."
>
> Strategy – Slow down, breathe deeply, look at the person speaking, and check with them on your understanding of their position.
>
> Barrier - Interruptions
>
> Strategy - Close the door. Get away from your desk. Close down your computer; turn off your phones.

Barrier: _____

Strategy: _____

Barrier: _____

Strategy: _____

(b) In the "Listening" chapter we espouse the power of the LISTENING CHECK as a key method of improving your listening skill. A listening check is not a near verbatim regurgitation of the words you have just heard. It is your concise summary of your best understanding of the content and emotion of what you have just heard. If you say, "I just can't do this assignment. I've been up all night and I can't get it right." depending on your tone and countenance my listening check might be, "Sounds like you have been working really, really hard on this project, and have yet to figure it out. You sound tired and near the point of giving up." My summation may or may not be on target. The beauty of the listening check is that it gives you the opportunity to respond and clear up any misunderstanding thus enhancing the communication. You may respond by saying, "I am tired and at wits end, but I am not ready to give up. I need your help." Your listening checks also show empathy and send a clear message to the person that you are listening and that you care about what they have to say.

Using listening checks effectively takes practice. Work on the skill at home with family and at work with close trusted colleagues.

Resolve over the next 90 days to develop your "listening check" skills and solicit feedback on your listening ability. When you receive feedback, listen to it!

My 90-day LISTENING GOALS:

_____

_____

_____

CHAPTER TWELVE

CREATING VALUE

UNDERSTANDING

Clint Eastwood's "Dirty Harry" character is famous for his grizzly quote, "Go ahead, make my day." Far from the tone and intent of this movie statement, those you work with and attempt to serve really are waiting for you to make their day. One of our goals is to make somebody's day, everyday. In some simple way by showing appreciation, acknowledgement, gratitude, or recognition, we strive to make some team member's or some customer's day a great one. These simple acts are really easy to do, but it is also easy as a busy professional to get caught up in the world of taking care of our own day, missing the opportunities to lift up others.

We all have fundamental needs. Left to our own instincts, we might spend all of our energy each day seeking to meet our needs. As human beings, though, we have been given the capacity to see beyond ourselves and understand the needs of others. Ironically, we often find that through understanding and meeting the needs of others, we meet our own needs and enhance our own lives. We also learn that there are few more gratifying undertakings than helping others to reach their goals, solve their problems, or increase their business and personal success.

 The people you work with and for need to be heard and understood. They need to be acknowledged and praised for their contributions and successes. They need to be recognized for their good intentions. And they need to be told the truth with great consistency and compassion.

These principles are eloquently presented in a book by Hyler Bracey, Aubrey Sanford, Roy Trueblood and Jack Rosenbloom entitled, "Managing From the Heart." Their premise is that each of us has needs that they call "unspoken requests." The H.E.A.R.T. principles are worth remembering. The five principles describe each of these primary unspoken requests. If we can respond to these unspoken requests in our daily interactions with others, we will gain trust and influence in creating value with and through others. The "H." principle is, "Hear and Understand Me," recognizing that all individuals need to be valued. The "E." represents, "Even if you disagree with me; please don't make me wrong," suggesting that as you work with others you should be careful to distinguish their actions from their humanity. Even when we must correct others it is wise not to judge the person and to focus on clear, nonjudgmental feedback about the person's actions. The "A." stands for, "Acknowledge the greatness within me," recognizing our need for recognition and praise for our good work. Take time to catch people doing things well, and let them know about it. Affirming the strengths of others is a powerful tool in helping others find their way to self-confidence and success. The "R." unspoken request is, "Remember to look for my loving intentions," acknowledging that most folks you work with do not wake up in the morning intending to do less than good work. Be slow to judge and quick to look for the highest intentions, even when people let you down. The final principle, the "T." represents, "Tell me the truth with compassion." Deep down we all want to know the real truth, even when it stings. It is all too easy sometimes to tell others what we think they want to hear. However, the truth should not be used as a weapon, but rather delivered with caring and compassion. We heartily recommend these H.E.A.R.T. principles to you as you seek to show more understanding.

By being compassionate and having empathy for your team members and customers, you can and will be more responsive to their needs. What are your team members passionate about? What are your customers passionate about? How are you responsive to those passions? Do you really care about helping others be successful?

Joey had a lot of hard lessons in Right Tracking his career. *"Some of my biggest mistakes early in my career dealt with my strong focus on my personal goals, which did not involve enough teaching and helping others succeed. I was blinded by my perception that everyone had the same drive and burning desire to succeed. By being too focused on my personal goals, I did not demonstrate the understanding and compassion necessary to be an effective leader. So much more could have been accomplished if I had been more understanding and a better listener. Others won't follow you, unless they feel like you understand their needs, unless they feel like that they can trust you to help meet their needs, also."*

Beware of professional jealousy, recognize it for what it is and meet it with kindness. As you begin to track a successful career, unfortunately, you will encounter individuals who are not team players. You will discover situations where your perspective or feelings are ignored or overlooked. You may feel that your team members are not listening to you or are moving forward without your input. Rise above these challenges and continue to "Manage From The Heart."   Express your concerns very professionally and be forgiving.

Understanding requires empathy (walking a mile in another's shoes), caring and tolerance. It also requires a true appreciation of the full spectrum of the diversity of human strengths, styles and talents. On occasion, most of us slip into a "my way or the highway" mentality, adopting the notion that if you think, act, or see things differently than I do, you must be wrong. Patience, openness and a fundamental respect and appreciation for differing views mark true understanding and help keep us from remaining stuck in our way of thinking. Develop a deep resolve to be quick to listen and slow to judge. Adopt the Covey mentality. Actively seek "first to understand; then to be understood."

<u>UNDERSTANDING 90-DAY ACTION PLAN</u>

(a) Which of the following assertions best describe you.

1. I am a quick judge of character.
2. I grow impatient with differing opinions.
3. I am most comfortable around like-minded colleagues.
4. I enjoy a good debate, so long as I win it.
5. I learn the most when I listen best.
6. I actively seek to understand others' highest intentions.
7. I try to catch people doing things right and make sure they know it.
8. My best moments come when I can understand and affirm others.

Again, wherever you are on this list; resolve to move toward statements 5 through 8.

(b) As you develop your 90-day plan, set a goal around a specific client or two, and a couple of colleagues for whom you are willing to invest time and energy to better understand. Develop a specific strategy for each. Go ahead, make my day!

1. Client/customer _____

_____

Understanding strategy _____

_____

2. Colleague/team-mate _____

_____

Understanding strategy _____

_____

CHAPTER THIRTEEN

CREATING VALUE

Energy

Think about the last social event you attended. To whom did the crowd migrate? Usually, the crowd migrates to those individuals who demonstrate the most verve or animation. When you walk into a room does the energy level go up or go down? When you show up at the office for work in the mornings and interact with other team members, does the team gain energy or lose energy? Just like a positive attitude, high energy attracts people and creates more energy.

Now, not all of us are blessed with contagious charisma and an inherently energetic personality. But, even if those traits did not come to us naturally, we each have the ability to display more emotion, more energy and to share our passion. You should be very open about sharing your passion for your profession. This openness and passion has a very positive effect on team members and customers, bringing about its own kind of energy. Don't you enjoy working with someone who is passionate about what they are doing? Aren't passionate high-energy customers more interesting or fun to work with?

Even the voice mail message we leave on the phone system, tells everyone what our energy level is. The tone of your voice on the phone sends messages to everyone with whom you talk. Isn't it wonderful to get off the phone and feel like someone has just hooked you up to their energy source? On the other hand, how quickly do you try to get off the phone with someone who is draining all of your energy? Have you ever gotten voice mail before that was so low-energy; you decided to call someone else? An energetic, "Have a GREAT DAY" can put a smile into anyone's day. Using high energy in your communications makes you more effective.

 Energy is one of the keys to high performance. How many high performance professionals do you know that demonstrate a low-energy level? Most likely, there are none. Most of the more successful professionals are high-energy people. They may not always have the most charismatic personality, but they are full of energy and enthusiasm. Don't underestimate the power of energy.

One way you can capitalize on your energy level is to understand when you have high-energy periods and low periods. By understanding your ebbs and flows, you can better manage your interactions with others. You cannot be high energy all of the time so you need to structure those activities that require more energy around your most energetic times. Also understanding what activities generate energy and passion within you allows you to create energy by changing activities.

Your personal health physically, psychologically and spiritually, plays a big role in your energy level and your ability to be effective for long periods of time. Prioritize proper diet, exercise and rest. The "Right Career Track" always includes plenty of exercise. Busy professionals must work hard to prioritize this time. But ultimately, your success will depend in great part on your health. And, your health is far too important to compromise. Form good habits early and make sure exercise is part of your weekly routine.

ENERGY 90-DAY ACTION PLAN

Energy is as real in human interpersonal relations as it is in the physical world. Human energy is as real as the shining sun, as electricity, as the combustion engine. A lack of physical, psychological and/or spiritual energy is a very real limitation to achieving the goals you have committed to through the preceding 12 chapters. You will need a full tank to create rare value!

(a) Assess your own energy level on the dimensions below. (1-being running on empty; 10-being revved and ready to go). Get input from your family and team members before rating yourself.

                          Physical Energy   (1-10)
                          Mental Energy   (1-10)
                          Spiritual Energy   (1-10)

(b) Develop a 90-day game plan to increase your energy in each of these three dimensions.

Physical energy plan _____

Mental Energy plan   _____

Spiritual Energy   _____

(c) Identify what periods of the day you consistently display and have higher energy levels? Over the next 90 days how can you schedule important tasks into these high-energy periods?

High Energy Period   _____

Important Tasks   _____

FINAL THOUGHTS

Max Dupree said, *"We cannot become what we need to be by remaining what we are."* That pretty much sums up what this book is about - empowering yourself with a strong vision and action plan that challenges you to develop an uncommon focus, energy and resilience. By understanding the four areas of creating value (customer service, team development, marketing and innovation) and applying the thirteen principles described herein, you are already on the right track to achieve your goals. You truly are running your own company.

 *One's philosophy is not best expressed in works; it's expressed in the choices one makes. In the long run we shape our lives and we shape ourselves. The process never ends until we die. And the choices we make are ultimately our responsibility.*

-Eleanor Roosevelt

Get away from your comfort zone and be accountable to yourself and your future with the 90-day action plans. Challenge yourself to improve continuously and remain focused on your goals. Keep in mind that the toughest part of undertaking any new challenge is always taking the first step. In our space program, for each mission in space, the lift off expends more energy in the first mile or two than in the rest of the trip, which covers thousands of miles. Once you get started, though, the rest of the trip is much easier. You can do it. Maintain balance within your life and remember to prioritize God, Family and then your career. Be thankful each day for your blessings. You are unique and empowered to shape your life and career everyday.

Success is not accidental. It takes commitment and vision. Your decisions today will make a difference now and in your future. Everything you do, say and think has an impact on where you guide your company and career. Remember that successful professionals are willing to make the hard choices. And, success comes to those who are willing to stay committed and focused, as well as put forth extraordinary effort. Top performers are enthusiastic about what they do, and they exhibit a strong desire to achieve. This success and the sense of empowerment and autonomy you will enjoy from applying the principles of this book are among the greatest rewards of your professional career.

ABOUT THE AUTHORS

Joey D. Havens, CPA

Joey D. Havens, CPA is the Firmwide Director of Physician Services for Horne, LLP a regional CPA Firm with offices in Mississippi, Alabama, Tennessee and Louisiana. He serves on the Firm's Board of Directors and leads a team of health care consultants providing services to physicians, medical groups, hospitals, ambulatory surgery centers and other health care organizations as they develop strategies to meet today's market demands. He has been instrumental in the development and teaching of Horne's leadership program "Capstone" as well as served as mentor and coach for numerous professionals.

Joey is Co-Editor of Medical Management Advisor, a monthly electronic newsletter published by Windsor Professional Information. In 2002, the American Medical Association released Joey's book entitled "Physician Practice Mergers". He has also co-authored two other books entitled "Performing an Operational and Strategic Assessment for a Medical Practice" and "IPAs Claiming Larger Role in Health Care Delivery" published by John Wiley & Sons, Inc. He has published numerous articles in national, state and local publications and is frequently asked to speak on health care reform, physician compensation, strategic planning, and integration to both regional and national audiences. Joey served on the Advisory Committee of the Center for Research in Ambulatory Health Care Administration to publish Medical Group Practice Chart of Accounts, first edition, 1996. Joey was a recipient of the Mississippi Business Journal's 1996 "Top 40 Under 40" Leadership Award. He also is a participant in the AMA Doctor's Advisory Network.

Joey graduated from the University of Mississippi with a bachelor's degree in business administration, and in 1984 he joined Horne, LLP. His professional associations include memberships/affiliations in the National Association of Health Care Consultants, The Integrated Physicians Association of America, American Institute of Certified Public Accountants, and the Mississippi Society of Certified Public Accountants. He is an affiliate member of the Medical Group Management Association and a charter member of the National Association of Physician/Hospital Organizations.

Joey and his wife, the former Cathy Cole of Nathez, Mississippi, reside in Jackson, Mississippi. They have four children; Brandon, Haley, Kelsey and Rigby.

* * *

Dr. Joseph S.Paul

Dr. Joseph S. Paul has served more than 25 years as a University of Southern Mississippi student affairs administrator. Before becoming vice president for student affairs in February 1993, he held a variety of positions, including assistant director of student activities, assistant vice president and dean of student development. He also holds faculty rank in USM's College of Education and Psychology, teaching in the graduate program in educational leadership in addition to instructing a freshman leadership seminar. He has articles published in national periodicals and, in 1987, appeared on NBC's Today Show.

Beyond his work at Southern Miss, Paul has presented seminars and training in management and leadership for business, industry and education. He was a senior consultant with The Atlanta Consulting Group, a Fortune Top 50 management consulting firm. Clients Paul has worked with include UPS, RJR Nabisco, Ohio-Edison, Sanderson Farms, US Navy, Accenture and Horne CPA Health care group.

Paul holds a Ph.D. in administration of higher education from the University of Alabama and was named the university's Most Outstanding Doctoral Student in the field in 1985. The Bay St. Louis native earned a bachelor's degree in communication and political science from USM in 1975, graduating magna cum laude, and received a master's degree in communication and management from Southern Miss in 1978. He was inducted into the University of Southern Mississippi Alumni Hall of Fame in 2000.

In 1978, Paul was named the National Association of Student Personnel's Outstanding New Professional. In 1981, the Jaycees named him Mississippi's Outstanding Young Man. He is also a 1987 graduate of Leadership Mississippi training.

Among many civic activities Paul has served two terms as president of the United Way of Southeast Mississippi. He has also been president of the Hattiesburg Area Education Foundation, on the Board of Directors for the Hattiesburg Boys and Girls Club and has been a trustee for the Hattiesburg Public School District. He is co-founder of the Hattiesburg Leaders for a New Century program and has served on a statewide basis in leadership positions with the Mississippi Economic Council.

Paul, and his wife, the former Meg Pearson have two children. They are active members of Trinity Episcopal Church. They reside in Hattiesburg, Mississippi.